PERMIT ME TO WRITE MY OWN ENDING

REBECCA FAULKNER

WWW.WRITEBLOODYUK.CO.UK

First edition.
ISBN 978-1-8380332-6-2

Cover and Book Design by Angelo Maneage
Cover Photograph by Laura Fontaine
Edited and Proofread by Fern Beattie

Typeset in Bergamo and Andale Mono

Write Bloody UK • London, UK

Support Independent Presses
WWW.WRITEBLOODYUK.CO.UK

PERMIT ME TO WRITE MY OWN ENDING

CONTENTS

I KNOW THE SEA IS DEEP   11
TWELVE   15
HALF BROTHER   16
ROPE   17
BONFIRE NIGHT   18
OPERATION VIRGINITY   19
BEES   20
SIXTEEN   21
BRIGHTON BEACH   25
TRANSFERENCE   26
VIABLE   27
ARMISTICE   28
GOOD ENOUGH MOTHER   29
SMALL BODIES OF WATER   30
MOTHER'S RUIN   31
FIREWEED   35
SUNDAY BEST   36
THEY EXECUTED ME ON A BRIGHT AFTERNOON IN FEBRUARY   37
THERE'S ALWAYS A WAR ON   38
BLITZ SPIRIT   39
KING'S HEAD   40
NEXT OF KIN   41
EACH SLOW DUSK   42
LAUNDRY QUARTERS   45
SHRINK   46
FLIGHT   47
PERMIT ME TO WRITE MY OWN ENDING   48
DISAPPEARING FEMALE CHARACTER   49
MY SADNESS IS VERY PARTICULAR   50
KNOCK DOWN GINGER   51
MOTHER TONGUE   52
POSTPARTUM   53
HOOK   57
PREY   58

EIGHTEEN MONTHS CLEAN   59
ALEXANDERPLATZ   60
THE MONTH OF EMERGENCIES   61
TRAFALGAR SQUARE   62
ANNOTATED BIBLIOGRAPHY   63
ANOTHER WORD FOR VICTORY   64
CONDUIT   67
HARBOR ARM   68
CEMETERY CRUSH   69
DEPARTURES   70
YOU CAN'T ALWAYS GET WHAT YOU WANT   71
HANGMAN   72
ELEGY FOR TEENAGE GIRLS   73
WISHBONE   74
SAVAGE   75
LAST RITES   77

For my daughters –

It is a joy to be hidden but a disaster not to be found.

D.W. WINNICOTT

I KNOW THE SEA IS DEEP

& the shoreline keens & punches. Above me cops
trawl for clues. They find matchbooks at the cliff edge,
beat up Converse jilted in the heather.
Give 'em what they need, keep what you know.
I know your height, your street, my fingers shake,
you hated sports & liars & not being high. Limbs
loud like mixtapes, we grabbed fistfuls of skin at recess,
rolled your cigarettes, wore your jeans slung low
for late night dares, your eyes on me when you said yes
to the roiling kick & the depths of rooftop jumps
landing hard on concrete, wishing it were beach soft.
Gulls nudge & shriek as they wheel out the gurney
your feet twisted under polythene. The papers said
we climbed too far, that accidents happen.
But I was up there with you, like before.
I know you removed your shoes,
that your blond hair flew like a slap.

All childhood is an emigration.

TWELVE

Someone was in the house, in my room I tell the police. The summer
I turn 12, standing in the kitchen *Karate Kid* cocky. Fingers wild

with popsicle juice & the murder of flying ants, their bodies burst cranberry
on the wood parquet, antennae twitching like the Detective Inspector's right eye

when he looks at me. Doesn't know I was awake at 2am with the Honda humming
quiet clicks on the phone, the cord stretched under my door umbilical tight.

Should I tell him about the men who ask me to call them daddy? I lie in the yard
where we buried the cats thinking about crowbars & getaway cars, the speed & sweat

of forced entry. Suck my arm & count to ten, blood vessels swell. I know what thieves
leave behind. A sky bedsheet grey, wishbones from cold Sunday roasts & the plum tree

that gives no fruit. Bottles of Gordon's, toothfairy's tipple. Milk teeth rotting
beneath the pillow when she forgets to visit. Garlic smell of dinner parties & betrayal.

The ring with the ruby star that Dad twists beneath his knuckle. Mum lying awake
for years. They say I am too young to understand the value of what was stolen.

As the welt on my arm rises I am slick with the saliva of criminals.
Why didn't they take me too?

HALF BROTHER

It rained remember   we climbed

to the roof   took turns dying

       our bodies glistened

& shook   white lies

       from your tongue   I step

into your game   screaming

I get five lives! but you always win

Hold your breath   *count to ten*

take your clothes off   *run!*   I crawl

into your lap   your arms wide open

rooms   pinch skin at my elbow

       shout *chicken!*   I stumble

jeans damp   sky at our backs poking

       night sockets   I am itchy-curious

like worms you keep in a matchbox

       they crackle & writhe

as you set them alight   your eyes full

of candleflame   when you jump

you take my hand

       & the rooms with you

ROPE

I hear them taunting me in the pindrop quiet   *(three, six, nine, the goose drank wine)*

their jump-rope slap scattering sparrows

      on the gossiping grass   *(my auntie told her I kissed a soldier)*

girls from my solitary summer gather

in the driveway   Juicy Fruit & ankle socks   *(now she won't buy me a rubber dolly)*

they clap   to the rhythm of sneers

I wait on the corner with the mangy dog   *(slap your thighs and sing a little song)*

make myself scarce   dodge sharp bangs

      as she grabs my collar   *(they all went to heaven in a little rowboat)*

points at my scuffed shoes   laces frayed

      (jump in)

      I clasp fear with its leather rope

launch into the ring   mouth dry   *(the line broke, the monkey got choked)*

scraped knees ready   & knowing they will leave me

      when the game ends   *(my mama told me)*

      I reach into the abandon of autumn

BONFIRE NIGHT

I dye my hair gunpowder black
in the kitchen sink   scrub

the spuds   November raw
watch men outside   toasting treason

their charcoal fingers   kindle the sky
my mouth tastes of salt & vinegar crisps

Terry's braces lies I craft
          so boys pretend to like me

I want to tell her about Thursday bruises
but Mum says *raven hair*   *you look so pale*

I am cross-country brave   long-legged
& low-cut with the hustle of becoming

burn my book report   wash blood
from my underwear   in the girl's bathroom

chipped pipes & the water scalding
I dry my hands   try to forget

the alley behind the playground
leaves crackle when I kneel   their laughter

floods the storm drain   as flames lick
the windows

I suck sulphur from my hair
my tongue   an unlit match

OPERATION VIRGINITY

I don't want to bleed on my first deployment
wearing my innocence like his dog tags

close my eyes as the bathroom spins   tight grip
on my arm   hauling me up   the size of him

at the sink   wet hands on his fatigues
I try not to speak   remember to follow orders

kneel down   shut up   grit my teeth
on the damp mat   bombs are loud

but my shame is louder   he moans
& I imagine wounds I inflict on his skin

elbows sharp   my ribs an arsenal   suck
swallow   smile   *don't fuss*   he growls

I'm doing you a favor   I surrender to the cold tile
ready for the platoon that will come later

BEES

I haven't brushed my hair since you climbed
through the fence, your orange shorts shocking

against the smooth cheek of spring. We crushed
foxgloves, sucked cherry lollipops, didn't talk much.

Kicked the dirt & practised kissing, our mouths sticky.
Distracted you'd shout *3,2,1, readyornot!* & take off

across the field in search of something brighter. You found
the nest first, small but wide enough to push fingers into.

I shook as the first one landed on my tongue, wings reaching
for my throat, bees polishing the air black, a blazing happiness

with its horizon of pain. Arms pressed against bark, you skinned
your knee when you fell, dragging me down as the colony lurched

stinging like a length of rope, their legion of quick bodies burrowing
deep into my skin, chest humming inside my shirt where your hands

were careless, gaping words I could not hear. We ran hard, striking
at fear, *don't stop* you said as my legs buckled. When you grit your teeth

shook the final few from my hair, I could hear the sound of them
doing their best to survive, and of you, trying to love me.

SIXTEEN

Throwing stones at street lamps for a laugh
you cover my mouth & I scream when the glass
shatters, night smell of tobacco on your fingers.
At the bar you turn your back & I lose my place
forget the rules, me behind you, elbows in the ashtray
making promises with ice & a slice. If you buy the next round
walk me home in my suede pixie boots two sizes too small
we can chase down the night bus past the bridge where Wayne died
jumping trains. *Unlucky*, you say because you're wild & immortal.
But boys don't read signs they rewrite rules then vanish as dawn sidles up
leaving grass stains & blisters when the pubs empty. I walk the last mile alone
brass keys clasped between shaking fingers. The Galtymore club flashes
                                        MORE MORE
shamrock neon & four of them are cologne-drenched
at the corner, lurching hands grab my crotch my hair,
last orders before closing time gents. A smoke & quick grope
their laughter careening off my skin, I take my place, coat peeled open
as they make the last bus. *Lucky*, you would say with your back turned.
This is how it is.

You look like a perfect fit
for a girl in need of a tourniquet.

AIMEE MANN

BRIGHTON BEACH

when the cab hits 50 I am on the backseat
counting contractions   as sunrise rips
through treetops in East River Park

breathing hard I am back at the club
where I held Jesse's hair   in the bathroom
the midwife takes my pulse

her too-thin wrists silver jangle   like Jesse's
that night we climbed stoplights
on Stanton   as my pitocin kicks in

Jesse's head on my shoulder
when we slept on the F   rode it out
to tomorrow   ate borscht

from chipped bowls   crimson
& cold   her breath sour from the pills
last night's heartbreak

on the boardwalk   Jesse showed me
the shape of her grief   how she slipped
beneath floorboards when her father

wiped off the blood   sandblown we skimmed
stones opened up slowly   she told me
it was time   that I should push hard

my daughter was born the night
Jesse died   I hold her small wrists
blue eyes open like morning street lamps

TRANSFERENCE

Little girls are hard as marbles you say
waiting for me to lie down   my petticoat caught

in your pipe smoke   hysteria is my pantomime
a tiny act of vengeance I speak   you listen

perform my heroic exploits   *How does it feel*
to be fourteen? you ask   childhood is ancient

Doctor   & I am done with the schoolyard
your words are a ceiling   I hang myself

by your adjectives   *Tell me the taste*
of your dreams I give you what you need

I want to marry papa   pluck all my brother's
feathers   cram them in my mouth

but truth hides in the folds of your couch   Doctor
desire with its glass eye spins from your notebook

my skin clock chimes   the hour   you are not
my father   & I am not myself

for Dora

VIABLE

I lost my appetite   bled
through wool tights   cut
my teeth on white
          plastic chairs
in the waiting room   crouched
beneath   my shame   deep
as the hospital sink   dodged
          ticking clocks
& your eyes at the door urging
patience   while the nurse empties
the mess I've made
          of motherhood

ARMISTICE

there are pieces of me   in the bedroom
ribs exposed   eyes rolled back

battle scarred   between the sheets
surrender my armor   to the August heat

limbs loll   metal & sweat   wait for you
to dismount   oil my aching joints

where tin chafes bare thighs   strip
my bandages   I wave the white flag

you speak of truces   tell me about survival
ready yourself   to leave me   I listen

it's better when I don't talk
visor down   helmet heavy

I'm a trooper you say   ripe for rescue
I gather myself into my throat

stagger back toward the trenches
this is what I am made of

GOOD ENOUGH MOTHER

neither good   nor bad
       I am your transition
I exist   so you can live
     in two   worlds
I have no free will   I meet
blame   naturally
     so the baby   begins
I can look   & see
     tell me
        am I enough?

for D.W. Winnicott

SMALL BODIES OF WATER

I tried to stay afloat the summer I lost the baby

stood on the shore   held the undertow

in the crook of my arm   rocked it gently

felt the water latch   cleaned the algae

from her slick black hair   listened for marshy

quickenings   when I'd swaddled

the small slippery body   on the lake bed

      I let the current claim me

MOTHER'S RUIN

I come apart   in the delivery room
ten days late   & sucking ice
my spine flooded   clawing
the needle   ragged breaths
cement thighs   I am drunk on fear
hissing for my mother   for a nurse
to pull you out   I close my lids
when the crow lands   blue pill
in her talons   wings muffle
your scarlet screech   she drains
blood from my womb & we soar

through a January wind   my neighbor
half-clothed   suitcases in the hallway
she is leaving her baby   whispers crow
beak brushing my ankles   the child's eyes
wild   *he has no socks* I say   taking her son
in my arms   my hair curled in his fist
I know what it is to want   to run   to cower
in the dark barn   palms in the dirt
I tell her   sometimes the branches will hold you
          there are days you will be less afraid
& as crow unfolds the sky   we mother
ourselves into morning

The work of memory collapses time.

WALTER BENJAMIN

FIREWEED

On the 26th night of bombardment I shake
the stench of gas from brocade curtains

wipe brick dust from porcelain
contemplate gingerbread baked without eggs

        at the all-clear
every stem in the garden has its neck broken

from the safety of the patio we watch
the evening shuffle in   a nightgown dances

in the hedgerow   poplars painted pitch black
        I want to tell you about your son

his freckles the color of burnt straw
about fireweed crouched in the dust of the dead

        their magenta spires resolute
nudging cracks in next door's fence

but there is no more room inside your busted skull for us

only silence and burning fuselage
        on the far edge of an ocean

your feet crumpled against the cockpit
as the air empties   I watch weeds lay low

their roots breathe in   and out
        while I light the stove

SUNDAY BEST

We shiver in Southend's gin-sodden drizzle, pick my cuticle
my tongue marzipan thick. Gran languishes in the ashtray

blue rinse set for tea on best china. Her flat smells of pets
long dead & husbands, wrinkled like the fivers she sends

at Christmas. I savor the rind of marmalade, half-smoked
Dunhills rationed on the hour. *I danced a foxtrot in my heyday*

those nights on the pier all satin & sparkles, she hung on
like hydrangeas, in spite of frost. *Don't pack me off,* her breath

a nylon crackle. But we didn't stop the movers that March morning
my patent leathers tight, slippy on the carpet of ward B

the place for wayward women. Mum said *be polite, tell her about school*
Brine-soaked Gran, words eaten by doctors with battle lines drawn

rusted spells & shoulders brusque. I want to shake her back
to the ballroom, bellow in her good ear – *let's go out in our frocks!*

We can drive a long nail through bleach, unlock tangled roots
& mildew. As the days shrivel she'd tell me about men

with shellshock smiles, women who endure. But I sat –
looking & not looking at death – closing the door tight.

THEY EXECUTED ME ON A BRIGHT AFTERNOON IN FEBRUARY

& the sky was silent as my brother wept
Thousands among us dissent
but the sun is weary & does not wait
Gestapo at our throats scream
high treason, perspire in empty
corridors at the knife edge of defeat, flirt
with a cowardly mob who close
their ears to the crack of a blade brisk as air
meeting skin, who continue to shop & drink
& fuck on such a fine sunny day
Who among us is ashamed? My skull
severed cleanly with spring crouching low
Hair knotted in the stocks, my words
rush forward, catching the light

for Sophie Scholl, 1921-1943

THERE'S ALWAYS A WAR ON

Seven weeks I've lived among dandelions, evacuee
in the rafters. No longer afraid of dormice scuttle

long grass quiet. I taste fear in the country lanes
liquorice-black. *No bombers here Mum says, not like London.*

She doesn't know I watched the Yarnton boys push
my brother in the marsh, lip split, knees muddied.

He cried *I want to go home where there's no mud and bullies
no "Chin up, son, there's a war on."* Nights underground

at Leytonstone, sirens close as bodies. Stewed tea and scullery
nylons - there's always a war on. Reunion smiles, a ragtag

homecoming brigade at the old Flats. Dad at the station
to meet us, his fingers grip my shoulder, smoke from his pipe

makes my eyes sting. Our street hung with bunting, white
wings earnest in their relief, brushing chestnut candles

in the courtyard, late spring yellow like warm beer. That night
we play in rubber tires with Hitler on the bonfire. Mum cries

when Big Ben chimes, their victory waltz rowdy and scattershot
smoke from Dad's pipe cracklyquiet. High up in the embers

beyond the city's rubble, I see a sniper in the long grass, his face like Dad's.
Evacuee among the dandelion clocks - my breath would send them soaring.

BLITZ SPIRIT

after Stephen Spender

Give me a death I don't have to endure and bury me
at Whitechapel, near the Italian café where you offered
to kiss me, then pocketed the silver. *Desperate times* you said

before bolting underground, blunt knives up your sleeve.
I should know better than to wait for you beneath crumbling
plaster from the rain last March when you promised to leave her.

Hiding despair under the mat, my keys chatter, the flat cold
like a hearse. Go back to her and she'll cover the cracks, polish
cutlery as the wireless clamors with horrors postponed.

Is this what you meant by resolve? Birch trees in the square
grey with rubble, pale knees of children scuffling while
the sky thunders. Your ghost curling the wallpaper.

I'll throw the keys in the river at Limehouse as the day
lumbers on, boil the kettle till it bleeds. When the ceiling
surrenders, let's scorch everything we couldn't save.

KING'S HEAD

midmorning & teachers can keep their history
lessons too tight classrooms   gum hardened

desks   & their corduroy eyes on the long haired girls
there are tanks in Tiananmen Square   students

with chisels climb the Berlin Wall   & the boys
are playing pool at the King's Head   I want to remember

lighting firecrackers on train tracks   nailing
the punchline on the top deck of a blazing bus

roaring past men   streets thick with their leering
but mostly I'll remember your forearms

when you line up the 8 ball   punchdrunk
I wait by the barstools clasp the nub of blue

chalk in my fist   lager shandies twisting
on an empty stomach   did the rebel in the white shirt

feel small   facing down men in chambers of steel?
or did he climb the tank with his grocery bags & whisper

my turn

NEXT OF KIN

our granddad fought the Germans but I battled through lunches

my bloodline gathered in the kitchen   uncles with 5 o' clock

shadows mistake me for schoolgirls they lured with pocketmoney

& promises   I pull myself together in their pipe smoke

arrange tins of beans in jaunty pyramids   kick shins of cousins

beneath the table   their tree bark cheeks ruddy   passing the sauce

as past lives lurch across history's headland victories chipper & hard-won

I want to start fires in the bathroom   wear the alley like a cat in heat

upend the garbage   take off my clothes   swear like a trooper

slice my thumb with the carving knife mop the blood with my bread

          but I *please&thankyou* my way through dessert

impossible   the things we don't say to one another

          stewing like spoiled fruit & cream

EACH SLOW DUSK

I toss a shilling in the Serpentine
from the shallows   grey voices

of the dead frighten carp   nibbling
at the day   there is no end to it

this murmuring of hours   in my scuffed
brogues I scrawl   on yellowed envelopes

          I do not want to die

setting it down as the artillery fires   & fires
I will go mad remembering

trembling   my laces tied with pond scum
fingers clasping   vines twisted in his hair

the cadet with missing teeth   reading Keats
          while flames lick the escalator

at Regents Park tube   everyone gives up
          something   & I am not afraid

to be alone   with the broken bannister
stacking clean plates neatly   after she leaves

I will open the window wide   usher in the dead
from Thessaly   Flanders   Belsen & Baghdad

we will sit & watch   a girl crossing the square
in a green dress   the trees alive with nightingales

for Septimus Smith

What we do not possess belongs to us.

FLEUR JAEGGY

LAUNDRY QUARTERS

My brother drove his car barefoot
the dash strewn with empties
old cassettes   and maps to places
he never saw   the sharp bend
how the river leapt
        and no-one said suicide

        but if you'd picked up
        as I fumbled laundry quarters
        for the payphone
        I would've told you
        endings are brutal

metal on granite
barely time to reconsider
before the sun slips
and silence
        steals the color

        so I let it ring   hung up
        when your wife answered
        my greyblue yearning
        twisting
        through the dial tone

like childhood drives
from the old house   wrestling boredom
and tuna sandwiches
my little brother's head in my lap
shoes off   sweaty palms on my jeans
wiping crumbs   confusion
when I woke him   relief when I whispered
we're here, we're here

        The rain tastes of gas
        when they haul his station wagon
        onto the bank   one headlight blinking
        wildly   I watch clouds destroy themselves
        listen to the hum of phone wires
        wait for you to answer to whisper
        I'm here, I'm here

SHRINK

I spot my therapist in the produce aisle, her fingers

in the beets. Our eyes meet as she reaches for asparagus

I look away fast – like meeting your dentist at Al-Anon

an ex-lover at a PTA meeting. She should be sitting in her office

her long legs folded beneath her, offering me a Kleenex

I want protection – glide of the elevator in the afternoon hush

my saffron yellow chair with deep cushions where I bury shame

and find loose change. The way her hazel eyes hold mine

But here is my pain laid bare among bulk items and I am a child again

demanding candy at the checkout. Perhaps I will accost her, my mascara

running. She avoids my gaze, checks her list, gives me a pint-sized smile

I gather myself by the dairy counter, grasping for courage

and Greek yogurt. Listen to her heels on linoleum as she bolts for the exit

lose myself in leafy greens – two for the price of one

FLIGHT

stumbling in the halflight   when my friend calls

to tell me her mother is dying   just weeks left

the ash tree bristling with unruly finches   her voice soft

brushing white contrails in a cobalt sky   my breath unspooling

decades from her teenage bedroom   a late-night frenzy

of Dr Pepper bubbles   drunk on plush carpets & practice kissing

our laughter interrupted by her mother   *come quick!*

look at the birds with their golden coats   we ignored her

standing by the window   grey hair pinned back   gazing out

as wings beat hard in a scrap of blue

PERMIT ME TO WRITE MY OWN ENDING

I will tell you a secret as you burn through your journey,
thirsty & thankless: I used to watch you in the mirror
plotting conquests in your Levis, your shirt unbuttoned

for the revolution. Airmail envelopes buried in drawers,
a maze of years collapsing with each infidelity, your reflection
ordering me to trust you. But I am tired of your real skin,

of history & its thickening red voice. Ink on your fingers
& girls in your crosshairs, I taste abandon in the bite
of your cologne. Now it is spring - permit me

to write my own ending. Tonight I will slip out the back,
no longer witness to your misadventures, their gap teeth
& low-cut blouses & you, stray dog, your drooling jaws

open wide, reaching into your new decade. I have closed
myself before, a kitchen in midwinter. But I refuse to wait
with the cat that sits on the balcony, urging me to leave.

You will find ash where I burned your clothes.

DISAPPEARING FEMALE CHARACTER

Imagine the gaggle of press clamoring outside our house the day I disappear
for good. Neighbors will throng the cul-du-sac, burnt toast breath & tatty
slippers in the brake lights. Mum will go spare, give reporters last year's
school photo of me in my ribbed navy sweater *she wore it day-in & day-out*
In June I lay down, my stomach gnawing red & oily & the vanishing began
my feet tingled at first, exquisitely painful. With fading fingers I folded damp
laundry, smoked on the window ledge, elbows sharp. While Mum made scramble
I asked my calves to stop dissolving, waited for someone to notice the budding
curve of my hips. I was only hibernating, developing my female character
Who would I become from a glossy selection of magazine role models? Shrinking
Alice in my stifling rabbit hole, glamor girl or pixie waif? Royal princess with dirty
secrets. Four-eyed clever clogs. Filthy slag. I buried my options with eggshells
in my bookbag, dreaming I had no body to answer to. That autumn I lived
in the thin space behind the patio where the worms crawl, knees in the dirt
where crying felt like floating. My trunk winnowing, the top of my head small
& vague. I peeked out from behind the rhododendron as the search party
formed, Mum up front, her robe pulled tight. They'll find pieces of me in the yard
my spindly legs scaring the magpies. Maybe I'll surprise everyone & slink
beneath the door jamb, reappear in someone else's kitchen, self-assured
in another girl's body. I wonder what it's like to stride through morning
in shoes that fit. Deal your hand and always play the Queen.

MY SADNESS IS VERY PARTICULAR

I hadn't been crying   I'd been chopping

onions & you happened   to stop by unannounced

& sat with the afternoon light   behind you   on the red

chair by the stove   I remember your scarf   wrapped twice

around my neck on the Central Line   I held my swollen stomach

felt first kicks   & fresh strawberries we bought already softening

You missed your stop so I waited on the platform   watched the feet

of strangers   my neck warm & itchy   like regret that settles

I used to save small relics   wedding rings   death certificates

& letters to an unborn baby   I couldn't save   I tried to tell you

the Cornflakes box was too tall for the shelf   dented where I push

too hard   to make things fit   When you closed

the hospital door quietly   after the doctor said *it's gone*

when we ran out   of milk   my hunger

for things that are just out of reach

KNOCK DOWN GINGER

I spend August burning
toast   gazing at a plateful of blue

sky beyond the kitchen window
piercing joy of a filthy tennis ball

        soaring toward the net
curtains   where I wait

for the doorbell chime
with the promise of playing out

turning cartwheels in the touchy air
peals of laughter at the playground

instead of sliding downstairs   bruised
knees wrapped in threadbare sheets

eye holes cut   I ward off cellar specters
throw conkers at next door's gnomes

blistered fingers from our rusted
jungle gym   at teatime

the street reveals its wounds
grasshoppers thrum   I chase

the last weeks thin   listen
for the thwack of the neon ball

its owner vanished   back indoors
I find a field mouse   dead behind the stove

tiny paws curled tight   pink eyes bulge
my heart skips   kiss its matted fur

      promise to love it
when no-one else will touch it

MOTHER TONGUE

She is mine – my daughter
in a few days she will go
long shadows, human & fragile
measuring flour & sand, miles & tongues
with hands that make and consume. I am
folding inward, her sustenance, my hunger
butter & eggs, the yolk separated, salt
& the taste of belonging. Unwrapped
this cake will smell like home,
turmeric bold. It will bring no ill will
a ritual offering, my sacrifice

After breakfast, with papers
in order & the tarmac hot, I wash
the last dish, the fragrance of limbs
citrus bright. At the airport
miles & tongues, our hurried
goodbyes, no longer a child but mine
still. She calls me when she lands, her voice
distant & raw. I learn the cake was lost
at the border. With his knife the guard
sliced it into human halves, golden & fragile
I wonder if he ate it or if ants claimed it

POSTPARTUM

knuckles pram–raw   I wait   patient
in the post office   *tsk* at spring

        lumbering down the high street
tipsy & over–eager   like my mother

she would raise a fuss   call the manager
make a scene   in the package aisle

my abdomen tugs   reminding me
       Mum never hid her body

or her broken heart   I doggypaddled
       while she dipped crimson toes

lounged poolside in a green bikini
her Cesarean scar threaded with intrigue

but I stand & stand   my mouth barren
       nipples leaking quietly as I finger

passport forms   perhaps I'll be buoyant
       by July   I reach the front

as the grille slams   *position closed*
       my baby's eyelids flutter & I know

part of my life has ended   dust on the counter
slipping in the deep end   my mother

turning back   for a second   then swimming
a slow breaststroke away from me

Had to get the train from Potsdamer Platz
Just walking the dead.

DAVID BOWIE

HOOK

buy me a last drink   something cold
& neat   take me

through the lobby with the knowing
lamps just lit   pry me loose

a stuck penny   I'll wipe my boots
on your nagging doubt   & later when you lace

your shoes   overtip the maid vanish like fog
my fingers will invent you   on hotel stationary   crisp

lined paper shoulders   eyes black as my fountain pen
hours pass   sometimes weeks   I wait

for the hum of the elevator   click of the key card
do you hear the acorns dropping on the roof?

knocking   like caught fish   I am barrel-bound
my knees against   my mouth   open for the hook

you roll your sleeves up   this is work
the fragile casting of the line   our small acts of betrayal

I sit with the ice cubes melting   what I wanted never mattered

PREY

a handful of hangers on   at the wake

uncles shabby in black   & that kestrel is back

perched on the fence   near the wet washing   judging

the mud on my dress shoes   my arms full

of finger sandwiches   & the toll   of church bells

behind me   muted cries from the schoolyard

a Monday breeze   as I whisper   before the casket

there is no-one to blame   for rain at the funeral

for a son's share of an inheritance   his sister polishing

silver in the cellar   her fingers clasped in prayer

no harm believing   this is what Mum wanted

before she shuffled off   her possessions picked over

a carriage clock   candlesticks   sunbleached on the mantle

carving up the curtains   crimson thread clinging to the knife

through the kitchen window   I hear the falcon drag its dead

onto the grass   crying   first in hunger   then in triumph

EIGHTEEN MONTHS CLEAN

your sponsor said   did I not know

all those weeks   imagining you

dead on a beach   starving in a garret

blotting out miles of your life   when he tells me

you moved on   bought a house   sweat springs

in patches on his peach polo shirt   hairs on my arm

flourish from the force of your name   spoken so casually

the stairwell spins   I did not know

but I remember ~~everything~~   your stupid beautiful face

saplings bending   how a person can disappear

& the breeze can just go on touching you

ALEXANDERPLATZ

Three sheets to a brittle wind, I am unhinged in East Berlin
burnt chalk taste of trams & your mouth doesn't stop until

Sascha shows us the Jewish cemetery where the roundups started
Thousands dead & broken glass from nights German kids drank

to forget their history. *This is how the end begins* you say as I stumble
through the tour, peel off to buy cigarettes & green nail polish from

the thrift store near Café Oren where waiters circle the periphery
arranging ghosts inside napkins. You claim center stage, take us hostage

with your history lesson. As I brace for impact on the bathroom floor
my past descends like Luftwaffe. I wish I'd never asked you to unbuckle

your belt, peel off my dress on the concrete steps, the river bloated
with murdered revolutionaries. Remember the detour? How I hid

stones in my pockets after you zipped up your pants, in case I needed
to drown myself. Now you give the orders, tell me what to read

which side to take in the struggle, while Sascha teaches us to curse
in German. Some mornings I pretend to sleep through the dawn raid

all fury & lockstep. I want to lay stones on your grave, but I line them up
on the sink, my pebble army watching over me as I stick two fingers down

my throat again. *This is how the end begins* – wanting to be remembered
& forgotten among tombstones, forging my own name with all that is broken

THE MONTH OF EMERGENCIES

7.9 inches of rain fell in Central Park last night
dead cicadas on the crosswalk   their bodies bunched

in brittle knots   sticky candy sky
bright with grief   branches submerged

by the weight of our silence   a letter unread
          a door closed firmly   & all at once

the red mailbox collapses   my house teeters
rafters yearn for sleep   weeping in fresh

darkness   as faith slips from us   I mourn
the certainty of the street lamp   folly of the old road
          & we cannot turn back

TRAFALGAR SQUARE

my first mistake was kissing you
at the riot/blood on stone steps
stained purple from headwounds
my lipstick smeared/bricks hurled
as the crowd swelled/we crouched
behind bronze/my body pressed
against lion's flanks/felt your sneer
& the pavement's tug/hoses slippery
tasting truncheons & broken glass
the air cracked/cops kettle/hooves
like trucks with boarded up faces
I didn't run/my first mistake
when the man screamed/his jaw
at the curb/dying to be close to you
to shelter in the clamor/cannons
from ships at my fingertips/I can keep us
safe/leave it to pigeons to fix the country
& that man's teeth/my first mistake
believing pain has a decade/men who serve
will protect/our bodies/made for ambulances
hoping you would take my hand/believing
there was something left to mend/my first mistake

ANNOTATED BIBLIOGRAPHY

1.

sitting nocturnal close

with our rope of brown hair, people mistake us for sisters. Foolishly
I believe we are something more, brimming & requited, hurling ourselves
at the weather. Let me guard the limestone wall I build around you. Let me
huddle in the romance of rickety plush stairs & no central heat, our flat
damp with pencils, an anarchy of chimney pots & great expectations. (*To die
by your side, the pleasure, the privilege is mine.*) After class we pull up the drawbridge
coffee gone cold, styrofoam soft & wet against my teeth

2.

outside the June air is fragrant

with piss & jasmine, but I draw lukewarm baths against the Yorkshire din
watch her run long fingers across crumbling spines of paperbacks, find
the page, the quote (*her body is the word*) in the tub she reads aloud in a voice
she calls Chaucerian, bawdy & bonkers. *You sound like Morrissey* I say & she
laughs & bangs her knee on the tap which hurts because she's so good
at accents & taking up space. Later I cook & overdo it (too much sauce
& music & looking)

3.

she has a way of making me feel

I don't live here (I am uninvited). We have separate beds but share my bed
& I never make a fuss. When rain floods the entryway , soaking the carpet
climbing the walls I let it seep through my socks into her room, hold it
(cautiously) between my toes, so cold (like a moat). It curls the pages
of *Beowulf* even though it's probably worth saving (but I don't). I stand
in the damage that I can't undo & she tells me to leave

4.

the flood (she says)

& the kitchen mess & my mates are a mess, but mostly me (I am) & she ties
up her hair & goes out for a fast bike ride (swerving hairpin turns). I sit
down my jeans soft & wet against my thighs. My fingers drip onto floorboards
& I think, *your body is not a word, your body is not the only word* & I rearrange
the books on her shelf & pitch forward slowly through the open window

ANOTHER WORD FOR VICTORY

Niko knew how to survive   I just lay there
wrapped in a blanket of yellowjackets

the winter he almost died   coughing blood
        into his sleeve on the Northern Line

IV drip   hospital hum   his mother's fingers
closed the heavy curtain at noon   he told me

about his family's journey   Lithuania
        to London   via Jo'burg   he missed

the desert   his father   how the disappointment
of a people   weighed heavy   he taught me

to endure frosts   harvest words   showed me
        how to carry my pain like a paper flag

his name meant victory in Russian   unyielding
iron-clad   & when his lungs thawed   he disappeared

for days   squandering dole money with dockers
chasing finches in Epping Forest   as they beat

a passage southward   he lay in the dirt   measuring
his life   the thicket behind him   coal-black wings

in the dark air   months later I wrote down his song
        played it every time it snowed

My favorite thing is to go where I've never been.

DIANE ARBUS

CONDUIT

Death is in the water
grey & lazy

    I fell in once
    as a child   my first act
    of slippery defiance
    mistaking silt & feathers for love

Death is leaking sewage
from the passageway

    I drifted   untethered
         hiss from the lock as it emptied
    screech from the aviary
            above

Death is spying
on lovers out for a stroll

    I sank slowly
        school shoes unbuckled
    the charred sky softening

Death is clawing
muddy fingers on the towpath

    I yielded to the canal bed
        my limbs tasting damp earth
    & forgetting

    I spat & kicked
    when he dragged me out
    biting the man

        his hero arms
    & wet mouth on mine

      Death in my lungs   I breathe in

HARBOR ARM

I have to leave   you said
that day on Folkestone pier
rain sulking through slats
like a dimly lit Danish film
you gave me a small piece of seaglass
worn at the edges   it was clear
you would go from the moment
you arrived   like a pilot
       light flickering
a glass of fizz at a garden party
a favorite Christmas ornament
my joy at finding you
       bright & sparkly
after years of overcooking suppers
while trying to rescue a moth
bumping against the kitchen wall
       door   ceiling
before sizzling on a bare bulb
my desire short lived & urgent
most of what you said that day
       was inaudible above
the weather   which whipped
       my hair cinematically
into a small child's face
so I couldn't reply when
you said   *I have to leave*
gripping glass   sharp
finger nail moons in my palm
       as I mouthed
It's very green   & far beyond
the buoys a beacon blinked
       once   twice
laying down blankets
for ships in distress

CEMETERY CRUSH

two sticks of spearmint gum loose
change in my denim cut-offs I destroy

September with my pedals calves pump
the hill's lip breeze blurs green then black

braking hard at the cemetery where we always meet

you're as vague as the avenue I crossed
tuck my face in tombstone sharp

we never lock our bikes you never say my name
but the dead are in my hair when your palms crush

the petals & babies who were loved briefly
cry out six feet below us rocked as the security

light stutters your mouth restless fumbling gravel
I give up my skin leaving sneaker treads & silver

wrappers with the dead who do not judge me

DEPARTURES

let's begin with his disappointment   he carries it
onto the platform with my suitcase   black strap biting

his fingers   I search for starlings weaving precarious homes
in rows of red brick   foolish & persistent   let's try to forget

the months he went down smooth as pills   we submerged
our doubts where the waves crested   but I clawed

the surface felt the shoreline tug   wanting to pick up the sea
       & show him how I am spun   from smoke I chased

other men I inhaled   he called me cheat so I pretended
I was honest   let's stop on the bench beneath the arrivals

my lies ladder heavy   I descend rung by rung   vowels catch
sentences lean   as he listens with his fists   steps away

to sit at the foot of my explanation   zips his jacket against the wind
rearranging the face of the station   he turns his collar up

extracts a mess of twigs   wooden slivers from my open mouth
       let's end here   facing rows of winter chimneys

when the train pulls out I haul my own bag as wings beat in formation
dumb birds   imagining they could leave   try to start over

YOU CAN'T ALWAYS GET WHAT YOU WANT

Fridays we play old Stones records in the heat
get wasted in the long grass at the reservoir

& the boys hit on us in clean Adidas with filthy
mouths   I keep one eye on the water's edge

one on Dan when he rips off his shirt   the magic
of being first in   Brian Jones was beautiful but

that's not how I want to go   face down in the deep end
one bloated lung & a rusty lounge chair   I want to stand

beneath a lightning struck tree   hold fast
as the power fails   kiss lips that fill my journal

lemonade eyes undressing me slowly   but I'll settle
for a summer of Stoli & swagger   my back against

a chain-link fence   another late show at the multiplex
sticky seats with his mates watching   knuckles grip aerosol cans

jerking   sinking   months of treading water
& drowning seems inevitable   come September I'll be the last
one standing   lift the needle & let it
                                        drop

HANGMAN

Feeling cheap as candle wax on red wine bottles
stale smokes & spare underwear in my pocket

your smell on my fingers as morning leans
across greasy formica. I sketch a short noose

on paper napkins, check my phone three times
but the 10:07 pulls in and you're not on it

so I amuse the waitress, subsist on sleeves
of Ritz crackers & stewed tea, thumb

library books I forgot to return, words placed
in the right order to make you miss me, tugging

obedience from something wild. I add feet
& fingers, scratch my stick arms with bloodshot

nails. Outside Bridge Street is squally, the fountain
plastered with pigeon shit. Remembering rain nudging

wonky blinds at your place, how light scribbled
every possible color. Sulking in seminar rooms

pretending I know less than you, desperate to slip
the noose. I finish my tea, crumple the gallows

there's ropeburn in your silence
& the cobblestones have their claws out

ELEGY FOR TEENAGE GIRLS

you won't always be this
sparse/stalking bathroom

stalls for kicks/while boys
with the sugar jump of soda

& fresh goatees/climb out
windows to break your fall

but finish fast/with a slow
shrug beneath the blue

garage light/it won't always be
fathers with mouths/vinegar

& twine/wrapped fist tight
staircases that smother/sometimes

you will be balling up the guts
of what was stolen/rending

the sky wide & cloudless
& sometimes you will wait
for the light/to change

WISHBONE

In the slumber after Sunday
lunch   my sister's on her feet   I scramble
to be always first   carnivorous
            in the kitchen   nimble fingers slip
for an even snap   too keen I cast off
dishes gravy stained   lunge for the greasy V
tempting luck   wrap my pinkie round its hook
            I can't grip   gristle caught beneath bitten
nails cold skin clings   I am cutthroat grasping
my brittle victory   but her nimble thumb twists
cartilage gives   I shove her hard against the table edge
wait for the crack   the tears   I am sick of scraps
            & being thirteen   too old for wishing

SAVAGE

hood up as rain knits the gutter   purling
the pavement where I pause   by the bus stop

pull keys from pockets of a worn out school day
sprint the alley steps   two at a time   touch

the chipped railing twice   (so no-one dies)
& that man is there again   under bunched up clouds

across from my front door   shirt untucked fly down
looking at me with his scrawny eyes   but I'm not scared

wipe my wet bangs   grip my backpack like Piggy
in that book we're reading in Mr Walker's class

boys on an island   hunting & killing   the usual thing
if I was in charge I'd lock all the men   in that abandoned house

at the end of the lane   haunted with dimly lit dares
& Friday kissing   I'd make them clean their rooms

get the washing in   there'd be no smoking
or spitting   & they'd always ask first

string em up & slit em dry, smash their glasses, make em cry
break their bones, jam their fly, I hope they die

eyes down to avoid   the pale worm crawling from his pants
I falter at the curb   double back fast

across the neighbor's yard   squat among brambles
who says I can't outwit shadows till supper?

line up my scented erasers   (so no-one dies)
I put the fat pink one in my mouth   strawberry

tastes like skin in wet grass   sharpen myself pencil ready
I know fear sits on the back steps   & death is a quiet house
          with the lights on

LAST RITES

Finally I figure out how best to kill him. Dead
weight on the kitchen floor, the night loaded.
When it's done I'll dig a man-size plot in the groin
of the garden, wedged between the broken fence
& eager clematis. I'll work the soil hard, deep
enough for ten men. Throw in my chipped teeth
and pulled hair, black nightshade, a bluejay feather
for luck. Scrawled notes and stale prayers, the cold
shoulder from next door. I'll sprinkle his eyelids
with shards from beer bottles hurled with the force
of a gale meeting my jaw, consequences that bruise
and swell. Spare keys from nights I locked him out
children in bed, itchy blankets smother their hot breath
while I heap earth on his body to keep him dead. I prefer
the slap of moonlit bracken, heft of a rusty shovel, my hands
bloodied. He deserves the worms, not the north facing sun
or horsechestnut shade. I'll wash him off me and plant
perennials, something bright that will flourish among weeds
next door's curtains threadbare from twitching. If they ask
I'll say it was the old tabby, the children's favorite. In spring
when the blossoms dance wildly, I'll scrub my fingernails clean
and invite the neighbors for tea.

ACKNOWLEDGMENTS

Writing this book would not have been possible without the love and support of so many people. Huge gratitude is owed to Write Bloody Press, and Fern Beattie for believing in me, and in these poems.

Thank you to The Constance Saltonstall Foundation for the Arts for awarding me a residency in 2021, where many of these poems took root and bloomed.

I owe a tremendous debt to my editor, Dr. Sarah Jefferis, for her unending support, strength and belief in me and my work.

If it wasn't for a pandemic, and the encouragement and guidance of Zac Furlough and the team at Passengers Journal, I wouldn't have begun sharing my poems with the world. Thank you for giving me the confidence to believe I had something to say, and for showing me how to sharpen the tools with which to say it.

Thank you to my dear friends who read these poems in earlier draft form.

There are so many incredible women in my life who have been anchors for me these past two years, providing me with quiet spaces to work, love, support and happy hour drinks. Special thanks is owed to Francesca Bell and fellow poets who have given me a home and a seat at the table.

It's safe to say that this journey would not have been nearly as electric without my frequent collaborator, artist and writer Pamela Crowe. Her strength, vision and solidarity has been transformative for me.

Finally, thank you to my family for recognizing this book for what it is: A lifetime's necessary labor.

And to Izzy, Sophie and Adam, for sharing with me the Winnicottian joys of being both hidden and found.

PUBLICATION NOTES

I am grateful to the editors of the following UK and North American journals where these poems first appeared, often in earlier versions –

"I know the sea is deep", *Pedestal Magazine* (USA), *Smoke Magazine* (UK)

"Twelve", *On the Seawall*

"Half Brother", *Ink, Sweat & Tears*

"Bonfire Night", *Rejected Lit Magazine*

"Bees", *Wild Roof Journal*

"Sixteen", *The Maine Review*

"Brighton Beach", *CV2 Magazine*

"Viable", *Literary Mama*

"Armistice", *Passengers Journal*

"Small Bodies of Water", "Postpartum", & "Mother's Ruin", anthologized in 'Rumors, Secrets and Lies: Poems about pregnancy abortion and choice', Anhinga Press

"Sunday Best", *Berkeley Poetry Review*

"They executed me on a bright afternoon in February", *Into the Void*

"There's Always a War On", *Footnote: A Literary Journal of History*, Alternating Current Press

"Each Slow Dusk", anthologized in 'Before the Cameras Leave Ukraine,' Black Spring Press Group

"Next of Kin", *Burningword Literary Journal*

"Laundry Quarters", *Solstice Literary Magazine*

"Permit me to write my own ending", *On the Seawall* (US) and anthologized in 'The Best New British & Irish Poets 2019-2021' Black Spring Press Group (UK)

"Alexanderplatz", *Prometheus Dreaming*

"The month of emergencies", *Writers Rebel*

"Another word for victory", *So It Goes Literary Journal*

"My sadness is very particular", *CALYX Press*

"Hook", *Midway Journal*

"Mother Tongue", *Passengers Journal*

"Conduit", *On the Seawall*

"Cemetery Crush", *New Note Magazine*

"Departures", *Honey Literary*

"You can't always get what you want", *New York Quarterly*

"Savage", *SWWIM*

"Last Rites", *Red Wheelbarrow Magazine*

REBECCA FAULKNER is a London-born poet based in Brooklyn, New York. She is the 2022 winner of Sand Hills Literary Magazine's National Poetry Contest and the 2021 Prometheus Unbound Poetry Competition. Her work has been anthologized in the Best New British and Irish Poets 2019-2021 and published in journals in the UK and USA. Rebecca was a 2021 Poetry Fellow at the Saltonstall Foundation for the Arts. She holds a BA in English Literature & Theatre Studies from the University of Leeds, and a Ph.D. from the University of London. She is currently at work on her second collection, exploring female identity and artistic endeavor.

www.rebeccafaulknerpoet.com

If you like Rebecca Faulkner, Rebecca Faulkner likes...

Counting Descent
Clint Smith

Small Machine
Demi Anter

Floating, Brilliant, Gone
Frannie Choi

Bloody beautiful books.

More Write Bloody UK Books

What We are Given — Ollie O' Neill

Ping! — Iain Whitely

Hard Summer — Francisca Matos

Small Machine — Demi Anter

The Cardbord Sublime — Oliver Sedano-Jones

Look How Alive — Lauren Hollingsworth-Smith